SAFE. HAPPY. LOVED.
SIMPLE SKILLS FOR YOUR RELATIONSHIP

ALSO BY LINDA NUSBAUM, LMFT

"HOW TO GET THERE FROM HERE"
A Guide For Marriage & Family Therapist Interns

SAFE
HAPPY
LOVED

SIMPLE SKILLS FOR YOUR RELATIONSHIP

LINDA NUSBAUM, LMFT
FOUNDER OF COUPLE MAPPING

1580 PUBLISHING

P

1580 Publishing
Published by 1580 Publishing
www.1580publishing.com

ISBN: 978-0-615-96715-8

For more informartion on Couple Mapping visit
www.counselinglongbeach.com

ACKNOWLEDGEMENTS

This book has been in the works for years as I have attempted to tell couples everywhere what I believe; that you can feel love and be loved in your relationships. I know in my heart I believe this because I feel loved in mine. I want to acknowledge the wonderful man who is my husband.

Even when we fight or disagree I know somewhere deep inside that I am loved by him and I am loveable. Sometimes it's hard and it's always worth it.

Thank you my man for being you. I am grateful for your support. I feel safe, happy, loved.

CONTENTS

INTRODUCTION   IX

ONE: WHY PEOPLE FIGHT   1
Bickering, sarcasm, nagging, defending, yelling,
threatening. It's what a lot of people do. Find
out why.

TWO: WHAT PEOPLE WANT IN A RELATIONSHIP   7
Everybody wants to feel LOVED. Find out how
we all end up wanting the same thing.

THREE: WHY IT'S SO HARD FOR PEOPLE TO GET   13
WHAT THEY WANT
Everyone runs into difficulties. Discover the
details of what happens in your relationship.

FOUR: OLD WAYS TO THINK ABOUT YOUR   19
RELATIONSHIP
You might be wondering why you aren't as happy
as you thought you would be. You might realize
some things you just expected to be true and
aren't.

FIVE: LEARN NEW WAYS TO GET WHAT YOU   31
WANT
Learn some new thoughts and begin to think
about your relationship differently. New
thoughts can bring about new behaviors,
responses and feelings.

SIX: DON'T BE AFRAID TO BE A BEGINNER   41
You don't have to be perfect when you start new
behaviors. No one is. You can always improve.

SEVEN: EVERYONE CAN LEARN NEW SKILLS   51
Understand at a deep level what you can take
control of to improve your relationship. Feel
better with your efforts.

EIGHT: ONE MORE THING   65
Reassurance for the journey you are on, a feelings
chart to begin to understand yourself and your
partner and something to remember when you've
had a big blow-up.

INTRODUCTION

If you are in a relationship you are after one thing... to feel loved. You want to feel safe, protected and happy. These are very human longings shared by most of us living on earth.

So what is preventing you from attaining these feelings with the person you are with? You may have asked yourself this question many times, seeking some kind of knowledge that would help you feel better in your relationship.

We all want to feel good with the person we love. That's just human nature. We want to be a happy couple and feel attached and not worry. We want to feel the bond and connection and just know that it's always going to feel this way.

Couples want to be happy. No two people decide to go into a relationship so they can become miserable. This is not how people think or act.

Two people begin a relationship to feel good. They each want to belong to something beautiful. So why do so many couples end up unhappy, wishing they felt better in their relationships?

As a couples counselor, I spend my time helping people repair and improve their relationships. It is possible to feel better and even feel close to the person you are with. It is possible to feel whole and satisfied in the relationship you are in. It takes courage, however, courage to look inside yourself and take responsibility for how you respond to your mate. It takes courage to risk looking foolish while putting into place new behaviors. It takes courage to walk through the muck in order to come out the other side to be happy. But I know it's possible to fix a relationship and make it better.

Unfortunately it's often the case that people in relationships end up misunderstanding each other, and these misunderstandings can lead to disagreements, arguments and fights. Fights can lead to cut-offs, or disconnecting from our special person, and this can lead to complete shut-downs where people just stop talking to the one they love.

These are common patterns that many couples deal with on a regular basis. Sometimes people get locked into a particular pattern and they can't get out of it. A couple can find themselves inside such a pattern and it could last for years. Then other behaviors start to happen. People get so upset at their mates because they feel so lonely and unloved that they may begin to really get mad at the other person and then they get resentful.

Some couples can live a long time like this; feeling resentful of their mate. When people feel resentful toward their partners they might pick fights with their mate. These fights have a lot of energy and get couples energized in ways that can mimick some sort of care. It does keep the couple engaged, but the engagement doesn't lead to tender, safe feelings from the heart.

As a relationship expert, the big question couples ask me is, "How do we get back to where we were?" Everyone remembers the early days when you met your beloved and think for the first time, "This is it!" Anyone who has been in a relationship can remember what this felt like. It's magic. It's amazing. It's the most wonderful feeling in the world.

Unfortunately it doesn't last. And I mean it doesn't last for anyone. Now you might be saying to yourself, what's the point of trying if I can't get it back? Good question. Here's my answer.

Relationships begin with great fire and intense connection between two people. That's how we choose a mate. The fire is created to connect us. Then the rest is up to us. This book is about helping you create what comes next. After the sparks wane, which it does in all relationships, it is time for the couple to learn something new about connecting.

Being good in relationships is not innate. This is not something like breathing. Being a good mate is a SKILL. And it's not that hard, but you do have to practice to be good at it. Think about all the skills you have learned in your life. I know you are good at a lot of things that you worked at. Your relationship is NO different.

This book is all about teaching you the simple, smart skills designed to get you loving your mate again. As a Marriage and Family Therapist I have counseled thousands of couples. I am now sharing what I know works in the therapy room with you. It's not rocket science, its practical knowledge. There is nothing secret in these pages. The information here about new skills is what I consider to be the essence of a good relationship building, and I've helped many couples learn them.

We all want to feel safe, loved and happy with the person we have chosen. We all want to have a sense of home. This feeling is beyond words and lives in the stuff that we all dream of. Here is your guidebook. Get going!

L.N.

1

WHY PEOPLE FIGHT

NO ONE GETS UP IN THE MORNING AND SAYS "I THINK I will have an argument with my beloved today." No one plans to have a disagreement. No one decides this is the best way to solve an issue. And yet, most of us resort to some sort of tactic to get our needs met that amounts to a fight with the one we love.

Why does this happen?

If we aren't planning it, why do so many of us get

trapped in the bickering, arguing, yelling and sometimes physical assaults when we are upset with someone we love?

The answer is just as complicated as the question. There are lots of reasons each of us get angry at the person we love. Sometimes we learn these behaviors when we are children. Sometimes we turn to them when we are unhappy. It's important to find out why we fight our mate. Some of us believe that if we know why we do it, we might be able to stop. That's what I thought once.

I love how human nature allows us to believe in ourselves at a very simple level. I thought that if I only knew why I yelled at others and couldn't get close to people, the information by itself would free me from my lifelong habit of getting mad at others. I really believed this. I was naïve. Sometimes we are beautifully innocent.

For me, I worked a long time understanding myself and learning what I thought about life when I was a child. I was often afraid. I bristled as being blamed or criticized so I stayed defensive. I decided the world was tough and would not accept me so I became combative and strong to survive. I thought that if I wasn't strong I would be hurt by someone or taken advantage of. I did not want any of that to happen so I continued to be strong and forceful as an adult.

I was fierce, and loud, and pushy. I usually got my way, but I spent a lot of time, in fact years wishing I hadn't made such messes. I crashed and burned so many relationships; friends, co-workers, boyfriends. Often I would feel really bad that I hurt someone's feelings. I even thought that they probably wouldn't forgive me and I had permanently damaged the relationship. Sometimes I did.

But it was different with family. I could argue and fight and get really mad at my siblings or my mother and they usually did the same with me. That was how I grew up. When you were upset, you yelled at the person who caused the upset. We all did it in the family. I think I was the loudest though. There were no cut-offs where one person said I can't ever talk to you again. No one ever left the family system and after a blow-up, and eventually there was order again. This pattern is what I learned as a little girl and it's what I used as an adult to navigate life. When I got upset I got mad. I was a "get mad" person. That's what I learned as a child.

As a relationship guide I work with lots of people who come from similar family patterns. Maybe you can identify with this situation. Maybe you had something like it in your home. Or maybe you had something very different.

Perhaps when you grew up, you weren't allowed to get mad. Maybe you weren't allowed to show any feelings at all. Maybe you were taught that the only feelings you could show were happy ones. Now as an adult you may be suffering because in addition to feeling happy, you also feel anger, and pain and loneliness and you don't know how to express it.

Regardless of what life skills we learned as children, as adults we bring them into our relationship with our partners. But it's possible to learn new skills to improve our current situation.

Now that we have established that our childhood experiences have an impact on how we interact with the person we love, it's time to put all this in perspective.

Even though it may seem like there are always reasons why you get mad at your mate, I want to let you know it's probably not what they have done; it's most likely because you need a new skill to tell the person what is important to you.

You don't have to understand every memory inside you to unlock the secret of you. Just taking stock that you want to do something different is enough to move you from here to there. Don't get me wrong, I am a big believer in self discovery. Why not look at how you think about things, but I also believe that you are fine just the way you are right now, and with new awareness and some skills you can become happier and a better mate to the person you love, without knowing every difficulty you ever faced in your life.

Anger is a natural reaction when we get our feelings hurt or we didn't get what we were expecting. Anger is a natural reaction to things. It's a feeling that can warn us with neon, flashing lights that something is terribly wrong. We need anger. Without our warning signals to help us navigate life we would be impaired, and we could be harmed.

So if you are like me and have spent some time being a pretty big expresser of your anger I want to invite you to look at your feelings of anger a little differently. You probably "hate" your anger right now. You might say to your mate, "I hate it when I get angry. I wish I could stop."

Your feelings about something that you wanted or needed or expected or hoped for have created the anger. Learning to understand you is the key to unlocking those angry feelings.

More on that coming up.

CHAPTER 2

WHAT PEOPLE WANT
IN A RELATIONSHIP

WE ALL WANT TO FEEL THAT CRAZY, WONDERFUL FEELINGS of LOVE. We want to freefall into another's arms and feel safe, loved and whole. This longing or dream is incredibly human and wonderful. So how do we learn about love?

As children we all grow up with ideas about love. Maybe we see it in our families with our parents holding hands or grabbing a kiss. We take in these images make assumptions about what goes into making up love.

A lot of our cartoons and our stories have happy endings with two people or animals falling in love. Family movies show us people loving each other. It's dreamy and wondrous.

Maybe someone we know talks to us about love. Maybe we read books about the subject or steal our sister's diary (I did) to find out about love. We are all curious. We know it has something to do with that other thing (sex) we're not supposed to hear about as children.

Chances are if you ever had "the talk" from a parent or guardian it went something like this; "You are a young man or woman now. You don't want to get or get someone pregnant." It might have been more elaborate with details about your body. But I'm pretty sure you did not learn a lot about love.

You might have heard something like "you'll know it when you feel it". Or, "it's amazing when it happens". I can just imagine though that those promises of future feelings were not very clear to you when you heard these words as a child.

How could they be? The person giving them probably wasn't very clear about the concept either. As a relationship specialist I work with lots of couples and they all have something in common. They all say they "love" each other. I've had couples use violence, or throw things, curse, leave the house, ignore the other and cheat on them. And in spite of these behaviors they all say the same thing, "We really love each other."

I believe them. I know they do. They just don't know how to treat their mate well and their destructive habits can fray and strain any relationship. Most people live with some kind of disappointment. Most couples have some level of intolerance toward their partner. Most couples complain to others about their mates. This is the state of happiness and love in many relationships.

You may be asking yourself, "am I happy enough?" Maybe you have accepted your circumstances and are just making peace with where you are; "I'm kind of happy". This is not uncommon. Most of us grow up wanting so much from our love-life. But the truth is no one is born knowing how to get it. No one has a built in rule book of how to create a wonderful happy life with the person they love. So if it helps knowing this, you are not alone. Most people live only half-way happy.

Look around your sphere of people. How many couples do you know that you would say are happy together? How many couples to do you interact with that don't bitch at each other or ignore each other or complain about the other? If you know one or two I would say you might have pretty good role models right in front of you.

But also ask yourself this, how many times have you been shocked when a couple you know separates? You might be someone who says to him or herself, "But they seemed so happy. I never saw them fight."

Often we are left wondering what happens to a lovely couple. I know I have thought these thoughts. When I was younger I idealized this older couple. Not too much older, just a couple of years. They seemed stable to me. They seemed happy and I always felt safe and comfortable around them, like the world could fall apart but if these two people were in my life I would be OK. And they separated. I was SHOCKED! How could that happen? I felt like I was punched in the gut. One of the people didn't want to be married anymore and wanted out. I felt so bad for the one who got left. I felt so wounded that this "ideal" couple was no more.

Losing this couple left me wondering about the longevity of anything; if they didn't make it, what then? What would that mean for me and my relationship when I found someone to love?

I think a lot of us lose faith and hope that anything in

the love department lasts. I don't think it's uncommon for most of us to believe that relationships are more likely to break than last. We just see so many break-ups in our lives. Maybe our parents were divorced or not living together. Maybe we experienced break-ups ourselves and lost hope of a lasting relationship. And it's easy to get caught up with the constant cycle of celebrity relationships and break-ups in our world. It's so pervasive, why wouldn't we think that relationships are bound to break? We would be odd if we actually thought something else.

Well not until I went to couple's counseling and then became a therapist, (twelve years ago) did I learn about being in a healthy, happy relationship. The most important word in the last sentence is LEARNED. I learned how to be a good mate to the person I love.

This is the part that is so difficult for many of us as adults. And I help people with this every day. What would it be like if you could learn the skills to be happy in your relationship? What would it feel like if you were actually at ease and relaxed in your relationship? These may be just concepts you think about at this point, just thoughts you are putting into your head as possibilities. Maybe this is something you dream about and want with all your heart. I believe they skills are teachable and can be learned. I have learned them. I teach them to others. How about you?

CHAPTER 3

WHY IT'S SO HARD FOR PEOPLE TO GET WHAT THEY WANT

FOR MANY OF US, GETTING INTO A RELATIONSHIP is a lot easier than making a relationship work. Falling in love feels just like it sounds: easy, just right, and natural. We forget ourselves and just jump in, feet first.

Falling for our person is one of the best experiences in our lives. It's everything, our ideas of happiness, our pictures of what love looks like and our thoughts of how our lives will be better and may be perfect from now on. It's just so great, it trumps everything that came before.

So why can't we always feel so terrific? Why do we start to see our partner as not so great and our relationship as lacking? Why does this happen? We might look at ourselves and determine that we are just bad at relationships. We might point to our mate and say that maybe we made the wrong choice.

So why does this happen? Here are some of the reasons. When we couple, we bring into the relationship all our hopes and dreams and desires. Each of us carries a lot of these ideas. We've actually been carrying them since we were little. All of us have thoughts and ideas of what a happy relationship looks like and is supposed to feel like. We have been filling our brains with these ideas since we were small. We get a lot of ideas from our parents.

Maybe we saw two people who really loved each other and we got a lot of messages about how to model our own relationship. But chances are most of us did not have perfect parents. Maybe we saw fighting, or unhappiness. The images of arguments get cemented inside our brains and that becomes part of a picture of what we think a relationship includes.

What ever we witnessed, those interactions are our very first ideas of what a relationship is supposed to contain. Then we add stories from our youth where everyone lives happily ever after. Add to that the media with all the images of what happy couples look like. And there are the schools, and religion, all with other messages about relationships and happiness to add to that mixture as well.

So each of us is loaded with a tremendous amount of hope to experience all the dreams we have stored. When we connect with our person, we carry all these images into the relationship. We fit our special person into our expectations and dreams and guess what? They fit!!!!!!!!!

That's what love feels like. A perfect fit. It's wonderful, delirious and engulfing. Only it doesn't last.

You may recognize yourself in the above description. Well here's something to think about, your mate has his or her own expectations and dreams that he or she has put you inside of. There still is a connection, and the two of you are probably right for each other, but no person can live entirely up to the expectations that the other has for them, and that's what people expect from their mate.

The first year and a half to two years, the ideas of togetherness seem to blend well. Sure there might be some disagreements, but they are not big enough to derail most relationships. So during this "honeymoon" period most couples overlook a lot of annoyances or disturbances. They just tell themselves, "Oh, it's not that bad." Everyone just moves on, clinging to the bliss that they had been experiencing. But every time there is a challenge, a little bit of that bliss diminishes.

As time continues, that relationship bliss continues to decrease and then other feelings start to creep in. We might begin to get irritated at our beloved. We might begin to feel bad that he or she didn't understand us.

These signs are perfectly normal, but when they occur many couples think other thoughts, like, "This may not be the right person after all," or "I still love them and I think I can change them."

Many couples enter into a phase that includes work of some kind; either working toward changing the other person, or becoming disappointed and turning negative toward the relationship. Some couples stay frozen in this zone for a long time, unaware of the difficult pattern they are in.

Everyone uses all the skills they have to get that bliss back in the relationship. Each partner tries to help the other see his or her point of view as to what's wrong.

Each one does their best to convince the other they are right.

Most couples end up suffering and blaming the other person or feeling bad about themselves. This cycle creates hardship for both partners.

Unfortunately, if you didn't learn how to understand your feelings and ask for what you want before you got involved in your relationship, chances of learning those skills on the job are very slim.

The truth is no one is good at relationships without learning how. We all assume that love is the only thing we need to make things work. I wish I could tell you this is so, but it's not. We all need some skills to understand our feelings. We also need to learn how to let our partner know those feelings without blaming the partner for causing them.

These are skills. They can be learned. By learning them you set yourself and your mate free of blame, accusations and disconnects. The difficulty in the relationship diminishes. It doesn't eliminate all problems, it just makes living with the person you love not something you have to avoid. When you have these skills the relationship becomes more fun because you have the confidence to know you can survive the missteps.

No one starts out with these skills, but every one who learns them can achieve what they have been hoping for, their relationship ideal.

CHAPTER 4

OLD WAYS TO THINK ABOUT YOUR RELATIONSHIP

WHEN WE ARE IN A GOOD RELATIONSHIP WE ARE IN THE middle of the best place we know. When the relationship hits difficulty some of us think maybe this is the wrong place and maybe we really aren't a good match.

OLD IDEAS ABOUT RELATIONSHIPS

- I am supposed to be happy all the time and if there is a problem then this relationship is in bad shape.
- In a good relationship people never fight.
- Everyone displays happy and good emotions only.
- No one displays anger or frustration.
- If I can't get a perfect relationship then there is something wrong with me or my partner.
- I work on myself or I work on my partner to make this relationship perfect.
- I am waiting for my partner to change.
- My partner won't do what I want.
- I am sad and unhappy and my relationship is not working.

Let's look at the old ideas and see if any apply to your current relationship.

I am supposed to be happy all the time and if there is a problem then this relationship is in bad shape.

This is a concept many people have about relationships. They are great when everything goes well. When things start to get sticky it's the relationship that's at fault.

Here's another way to think about a relationship. When you start and everything is great, that's a good beginning. When there are issues, that's an indication that you are being invited to figure out how to navigate the difficulty. The very first time you and your mate get stuck on an issue, you are getting a lot of information.

Let's say you get your feelings hurt and when that happens you stop talking and have to leave the room. This might be a pattern you have used all your life. Lots of people work this way, and it may seem to work. When you leave the situation, you feel a little better for a while. But it doesn't solve the problem and it could make things worse. Here's why. You probably will continue to think about what your mate did to hurt your feelings and this creates a pretty big story of how you felt you were wronged. This story becomes fixed and complete.

The next time you see your mate you will be ready to let them have it.

This is hard on you because you have to bring up the pain again and it's also really hard on your mate.

Let's look at what happens from your mate's perspective. You have just gotten up and left. You mate is sitting there maybe wondering what he or she did to upset you. The partner may start imagining all sorts of scenarios about what you might be thinking when you are mad. They also might be looking for what they said or did that caused such a big reaction.

Looking at this upset, you can see that both people suffer; the one who leaves and the one who got left. Both have a right to their feelings and no one is more right than the other.

But if you feel hurt, you might not see that your mate is also suffering. What you need is awareness of how your upset might impact him. And you might want to let him or her know that you didn't want to cause them pain.

When you think new thoughts about your relationship, you realize that you aren't the only one who has feelings. Your partner, who may not be able to show feelings as well as you, still has a right to his or her feelings regardless.

To be in a good, equal, long-lasting relationship, each person must feel that they matter...even in an argument. Both people have to know that their feelings matter, even when those feelings are raw and hard and difficult to talk about.

In a good relationship people never fight.

A lot of people think this. Many people believe that compatibility means never fighting or disagreeing. Some people live this way, but in my experience most people can't. People have feelings and sometimes they get misunderstood and feel upset.

The trick is to learn how to communicate even the slightest little hiccup in a constructive way. It doesn't have to be a big production; it could be something like, "Hey I want to talk with you about something that happened. I felt dismissed by you when you were sarcastic back there." Now that's not a big deal, but it might be very unpleasant to the person who felt dismissed. So if your partner brings up something, don't go into defending yourself, "Oh you know I was kidding," or criticizing, "You are so sensitive."

Just say "I am sorry I hurt your feelings." That's it. Those few words tell your partner who felt dismissed that you heard him or her; you understand what they told you and you realized that you were careless with your words and want to repair. You do so with a simple, "I'm sorry."

The partner feels better and you feel better because you got to repair them and they are now back to loving you.

Everyone shows happy and good emotions only.

If you live in a relationship where you just show a happy face to your mate you may be pretending. I am sure that you are not always happy. I am sure that sometimes you feel upset and disappointed. What do you do when you have these feelings? You may stuff them inside and not reveal them. If you do this you are keeping up a good front but you are not being true to yourself. Eventually you will grow tired of always showing up happy. You may even grow resentful to the person you were being happy for.

No one displays anger or frustration.

Maybe you live in a relationship where no one gets mad. This sounds like the previous segment. People who don't get mad do something with their mad feelings. No one has a life where everything is exactly as they expect, want and predict. People in our world get disappointed. This leads to frustration or anger. If people swallow their anger, or talk to someone outside the relationship about their anger to keep the union pristine, people begin to feel a sense of phoniness, like every one is acting. Nothing feels real.

Everyone on the outside thinks everything is great. People on the inside are pretending it is so.

If I can't get a perfect relationship then there is something wrong with me or my partner.

Some of us feel that if the relationship is bad it must be someone's fault; yours or your mate's. When difficulty starts to become more regular people start affixing blame. They either blame themselves or blame the other person or blame someone or some experience outside the relationship. Blame becomes the most common expression for people when they reach this state. Disappointment, frustration and anger become the fuel that leads partners to accuse each other of not doing the right thing. Lots of misunderstandings get chalked up to somebody not doing things well. Someone isn't doing their job right and that's a problem for the other. This leads to discontent. No improvements in the relationship can come from blaming the other for what is wrong about the relationship.

Think about it. When was the last time you decided

to improve your actions when someone was blaming you for something? Probably never. You might do it if it's a boss, but you wouldn't be happy about it. What makes you think that your mate will feel any differently?

It sucks to be criticized or told we are at fault. It just makes the person who hears it feel bad and unresponsive. Sometimes people defend themselves. The behaviors lead to discontent for both.

I work on my partner to make this relationship perfect.

Sometimes partners get the idea that if they could help their mate improve then everything would be great. This is a wonderful idea, but it usually lives in only one person's head and the person being worked on may not even know what they are supposed to do. No one wants to irritate their mate, (unless your relationship is really in a bad place). Most people want their mates to be happy. The problem with working on your mate is that he or she probably doesn't know what you want. If they do know what you want, you might want to inquire if your mate is willing to make the changes. After all, your mate has a right to his or her feelings too. Chances are if you ask, not demand, not threaten, and just ask lovingly, your mate would do many things to please you. Sometimes it is all in the asking.

I am waiting for my partner to change.

If you are in this category you are probably doing a lot of wishing and hoping and waiting. You are probably running out of good will because when we wait for something we often get exhausted. We worry about whether it will ever come and we might get frustrated and angry because we have been waiting for so long for things to be different. Unfortunately if you are waiting for your partner to change this is a waste of your time.

People only change when they want to. You can ask your mate to do something different, and register a comment when they don't do what you would like, but you can't make them be different. Your mate is responsible for his or her actions. You are responsible for how you feel about them. Let your mate know you would feel infinitely better if they would pick up their clothes, mow the lawn, buy the groceries… etc. Be specific and let them know what you would like. If they don't want to do it, you have just learned something about their motivation.

My partner won't do what I want.

Think back to your childhood when you became a thinking person. Did you always do what your parents and other adults wanted? Did you ever just want to do something different? Are you a parent? Do your children always do what you want? Do they ever express themselves with a difference of opinion? Give your partner a break. He or she is not on earth to make your life easier. Your mate is here to support you, but your partner is not your servant. Your partner is connected to you and bonded to your heart. Your love isn't measured by how many duties he or she carries out. Your relationship is based on how you feel about each other. Does it really matter that you don't think the duties are evenly divided? Is everything about fairness? "I do more then my mate," you might feel.

Tell them that you don't feel it's fair and ask them what they think? You might find out they agree or disagree. What ever you learn, ask for what you would like in a loving way. Don't' nag or criticize or compare. Ask with kindness, the way you would talk to a loved one, or a child.

I am sad and unhappy and my relationship is not working.

You probably have been living with these feelings for a while. You and your mate may have a behavior pattern that both of you have been able to tolerate. It isn't good, but it isn't so bad that you have to leave. Maybe you think about leaving. Maybe you think you could be happier with someone else. You stopped trying to connect with your mate because it's been so long since he or she has tried to really understand you.

You don't even know how long you have been sad, but you think it might have been for years. You don't know what to do because it's been so long since you felt close to your mate that you start thinking there is no way to fix this and it is probably over.

You don't talk about this to your mate. Maybe you mention it to a close friend but you keep them in confidence. You are afraid to talk about it. Your worst fears might be realized, that your mate wants out too. Both of you suffer. Both of you have been suffering for a long time.

You both have managed to survive the loss of intimacy and connection, but you both have become bitter and unhappy. This is a hard place to live, for both of you. And if you are reading this book a part of you wants to see if there is something you can do or feel to be happier. There is. Keep reading.

new
skills

CHAPTER 5

LEARN NEW WAYS TO GET WHAT YOU WANT

TO BE A GOOD PARTNER WE FIRST HAVE TO UNDERSTAND how many moving parts there are to a relationship. Most of us assume there are two; you and your mate. I believe there are three; you, your mate, and then the two of you as a pair. Like a three-legged stool: One part you, one part your partner and one part your relationship. As with a three-legged stool, if one part isn't strong, the stool is wobbly.

To bloom a truly happy partnership with lasting strength, each piece is an integral part of the equation. If one person absorbs too much energy, the other withers. If not enough attention is paid to the relationship itself, your partnership suffers.

Meeting Each Others' Needs

Many people believe that the only way to work on their relationship is to focus on the partner's happiness. The problem with looking at relationships this way is that the person trying to make sure their mate is doing well runs the risk of neglecting him- or herself. This person may be sacrificing what he or she wants or needs in the relationship so their partner will feel good.

That might work for a while, but eventually the person doing all the giving can run out of energy and feel exhausted and depleted. If this pattern continues, those feelings can turn into anger and resentment. If one partner feels like they are the giver and doesn't receive anything in return, he or she can end up feeling used and alone.

The receiver of this energy doesn't get his or her needs met either. He or she may be happy for a while, but this constant state of receiving can become tiresome, too. There is no room for real bonding between the two partners because their positions are not equal. There is imbalance in the relationship.

Meeting Your Own Needs

In a healthy relationship each person should learn about themselves as individuals. Part of self-knowledge is understanding what makes you mad, and what makes you happy. When you know this you can let your partner know what you would like or what you don't like.

Most of us know when we feel good and we can certainly identify when we don't, but understanding why we are reacting to our mate is key to a healthy relationship. Most of us were not taught about our feelings. Many of us just react to our partner when our feelings get hurt and we might even blame them for making us feel that way. When we have these reactions we are actually holding someone else responsible for our own feelings.

An important element in everyone's personal development is understanding why we get upset. What happens to us when we get our feelings hurt and noticing how we react. These pieces of information are vital to helping us navigate the relationship between ourselves and our mate.

So how do you begin? The first thing you do is just try and understand the concept so that you can understand yourself and figure out why you feel bad. That's the first step. If you can really take in that idea then you are open to the possibility of what might come next. You have just entered into self awareness. You have an awareness that you might be able to figure yourself out and feel better. This is the first step to real change.

The next step is to understand that you are not at fault for not knowing. I spent decades being mad at people who hurt my feelings. I probably learned this as a child and didn't spend anytime learning any other ways to cope with my feelings so I just continued in a cycle of everything is fine until it wasn't. Then I'd try and clean up the emotional mess I made and continue, until the next blowup.

Not until I met the man I wanted to build a life with did I really feel the need to change. I didn't want to crash and burn another relationship. I wanted this one to work. I had to look at my short fuse and my angry outbursts and figure out a better way to let him know when I was mad about something or got my feelings hurt. That was the beginning of my journey and I speak from experience that once you figure yourself out you will live without the anguish and stress you probably carry right now. You will be able to get rid of the hurt feelings and resentment you might still hold. You essentially become free, and that's where everyone wants to live… emotionally free.

So in my case I had to learn a very fundamental skill. I had to learn to **self-soothe**. Self-soothe looks like this. Imagine you are a parent of a five-year-old child. Your child falls down and skins a knee. You feel terrible and you cradle your child as she cries and you hold her and promise her she will be all right. This is teaching your child that she can rely on you. If you continue solving your child's difficulties the same way, taking care of all their pain, your kid will learn that someone is supposed to help them throughout their life. Your child will look outside of herself for answers to problems. Your child will not learn self-soothing skills. She won't know how to rely on herself.

Self-soothing scenario: Your child falls down and skins his knee. You say to the child, "Oh, I'm sorry you hurt yourself Johnny. You'll be OK." The child continues to cry and eventually stops, on his own. Every time there's a problem the parent tells the child he can figure it out, he will be OK. The child learns to look inside at his own resources to navigate life's obstacles. You have given your child the best chance at navigating his feelings and his choice of behaviors because he has learned that he can make a good decision on his own. You have taught him how to self-soothe. He can soothe himself and not rely on another or make someone else responsible.

This is a skill and an important one for every person and it will reveal the health of all relationships. Often times we believe it is our partner's duty to make us happy. No, it's our responsibility to know ourselves to be able to ask for what we want.

Another important tool to learn is how to take responsibility for our own actions and reactions. Here's what I mean. A long time ago before I was a therapist I had a good friend who was a therapist. I was lucky to get some casual therapy from her which I valued, she was a good listener. One time I had a fight with my Mother and I was venting to my therapist-friend about it and she asked me, "What was your piece in the argument?" Her question sounded like a foreign language. I didn't have any piece in the fight, it was my MOTHER"S fault. My Mother did something to ME! I was completely innocent.

Not until years later, after I had my own personal

therapy and became a therapist did I understand what belonged to me and what belonged to my mother. My Mother got upset with me and yelled, but my response, my yelling back at her, my action belonged to me. My reaction and upset belonged was mine and that was my "piece."

When there's an argument between two people it's hard to see anything clearly. An argument has its own power and people get lost in the challenge of fighting each other, it becomes a duel. In these cases it's harder to separate what belongs to you and what belongs to your partner.

But before the argument starts, there's a point where something happens to one person and then the upset begins. I am interested in what started the difficulty. That's the piece that belongs to you. All arguments are caused by someone not understanding something and deciding it means something else.

Think of all the arguments you have had with you mate. The first thing that happens before the argument begins is that you felt something. I imagine it's something like, misunderstood, sad, left out, ignored, dismissed, criticized, blamed or attacked. These are important things to notice. When something happens to you, figure out what happened. "I felt left out when my partner didn't ask me about my schedule before he made arrangements to go to dinner." That's separate from telling him what he did wrong. You want to figure out what happened to you.

Learn how you react when your feelings get hurt. Learn what you do, what action you take and discover how long you feel bad. This is your work to understand yourself. Once you know what happens to you, you can tell you partner.

Here's how to start. We don't want to look for answers while we are in the middle of a fight. The information gets revealed to us after it's over. So after you've been in a fight with your mate I want you to go to a quiet place and answer the following questions. This is a process just for you.

And you can answer these questions every time there is an upset between you and your mate. Think of your answers as the pathway to discovering the mystery of you. The more often you catalogue your answers the more information will be revealed to you about how you feel and how react. They don't have to be long answers, just descriptions to the following questions:

1. What happened to cause the upset? (Describe the concrete details, she said what, I responded, we ended up…)
2. My first feeling was _____. Here you refer to the feelings chart in the back of the book.
3. The intensity of that feeling (Rate the feeling 0 – 10, 10 being the most)
4. My immediate thought when the incident happened was, (Write down what you're your thoughts are. It doesn't matter what it sounds like, just write down your thinking.) Example: "I thought she was trying to undercut me." "I thought he said that to hurt me."
5. What you did, what action you took. (I locked myself in the bathroom. I yelled at my partner. I stopped talking.)

That's all you have to do to learn about yourself, to learn how you react, to learn as my friend asked, what is your "piece".

In a relationship there is your work, and there is the relationship work. This is your work. Become an expert on yourself. Know yourself. Free yourself.

CHAPTER 6

DON'T BE AFRAID TO BE A BEGINNER

WE HAVE COMMUNICATION PROBLEMS
HOW DO WE FIX THEM?

The most common challenge I hear couples talk about has to do with communication. When I work with couples I often hear one or both say this, "We just don't know how to communicate."

Chances are people in this situation also feel a lack of intimacy and sadness over being disconnected and frustrated. If you feel empty in your relationship and when you try and get your needs met you run into resistance from your mate, you could surmise that you and your partner are having communication problems. Many couples believe if they could just learn how to "communicate" the relationship would be better.

I wish it were that easy. I wish I could write you a chapter that outlined communication techniques and that would be all you would have to learn and then everything would be OK. But it's not that simple.

When I hear the word "communicate" I know that word is really code for "he or she doesn't listen to me," or "he or she doesn't understand me" or even "he or she doesn't love me because if they did, they would do what I needed and I wouldn't feel this way."

When people summarize their marriage or relationship strife as communication problems I know that communication issues just scratch the surface of what is not working between the couple. What I know is that it's not just a matter of learning different words to fix the communication problem, it's a matter of understanding what one is feeling and being able to convey it accurately so the partner can understand, much like we talked about in the last chapter.

Fixing a communication problem means getting two people on to the same page by helping the couple learn to be available for each other, and that usually means helping people develop their listening skills as well.

Most of us are pretty good at letting our partner know what we need, want, feel frustrated about, wish they wouldn't do etc. But how many of us are really good at listening to what our partner wants or needs or feels sad or frustrated about?

When we grow up we learn how to do a lot of things. We learn how to listen to our parents or tune them out. We might learn how to get attention by being a helper in the house or becoming a good student to receive praise. Maybe we acted out to get noticed. Whatever pattern we learned as a kid we probably still use as an adult. And why wouldn't we? We would have no reason to change if we are not in a relationship.

When we are with another person we are in such close contact our old ways of getting ourselves noticed or getting what we want or need don't always work anymore. This is no one's fault. Every one receives training as a single person when we are young and all of us do the best job we know how to do when we grow up and begin a relationship.

But while being dutiful or acting out might have been successful strategies before we were in a relationship, they just don't seem to work when we get close to another person. This business of not communicating comes in when two people want to be together but they get so frustrated trying to get their needs met and they just can't seem to understand why it's so challenging to make themselves heard by the other person.

There is a distinct difference between being an independent person in the relationship and being part of a couple. That doesn't mean you have to lose your identity, it just means you have to become aware of your partner and his or her needs as well as your own and try and think about both at the same time. That may sound like a lot of juggling, but if you learn how, then your relationship gets really good. When you notice what you need, and are aware of what your partner needs, both of you can get what you need and you are taking care of each other, seamlessly. That's true communication.

Here's a primer of how to talk to our partners so they can hear us.

All communication struggles can be boiled down to how something is presented. It might seem to you that you are saying everything in a way that your partner can hear easily, but you may be using words that make the listener feel like he or she is under attack or being blamed. The partner can't respond except to defend him or herself. That can lead to an argument and then everyone feels bad. Both people end up exhausted and spent, and the last thing they want to do is talk to each other.

It may sound silly to have to learn skills to talk to our partner, and it may make you feel funny and embarrassed. But guess what? These skills work!

The first thing we have to do is become familiar with what NOT to say. When you begin a sentence, here are the ways to make your partner see red.

1. DON'T SAY anything that starts with:

I don't want
I won't do
I'm not going to
I can't because
I refuse to

2. DON'T SAY anything that starts with:

You need to
You should do
You can't do
You must do
You aren't going to
You better not

3. DON'T SAY anything that starts with:

We need to
We should do
We have to
We could do
We're supposed to

4. DON'T SAY any sentences that start with

It can't be
Don't do this
Don't say that

When you start sentences with any phrases in the DON'T column the person speaking is already sending a challenging message to the partner. Starting a sentence with "I won't" or "I don't" tells the partner you don't like something and are already feeling an upset.

Anytime you start a sentence with a You, we are accusing someone of something. It feels like an attack or blame.

When you start your sentence with a We the speaker makes an assumption that the partner has already agreed to something. A "we" statement indicates to your mate that you are speaking for both people without the partners consent. "We" feels to the partner that they have been dismissed and maybe their feelings aren't important to you. The phrases starting with Don't do or Don't say, just feel bad. No one wants to hear someone who is already unhappy and is spreading their discontent.

So what do you do? Rephrase your commands and make them requests. Requests are without judgment. They are simply questions with content, nothing heavy. Start your sentences with the following phrases:

1. Any statements that start with:

I would like it if you would
I want to have you
I am happy when you
I am hopeful that you
I desire that you
I wish that we could
I am happy when
Here is what would make me happy

2. Any questions that start with:

Would you be willing
Are you open to
Would you like to
Can you join me in
Is it possible for you
Are you interested in
Would you enjoy

These kinds of statements have no blame or attack. They are coming from a place of wanting instead of unhappiness.

Try it with your partner. Practice these phrases together. Think of a topic you would like to discuss and try it out using the first series of statements. See how it feels. Try it on each other.

Using the same topic, now try the same subject using the second series of statements, and see how that feels. You just might feel different when you use the phrases in request form. You might feel more open toward your mate, less threatened, and safe.

When we are open we have a chance for true communication. That's when we feel safe enough to lay down our defenses. That's when we can have a true exchange with our partner. We might even learn something new about our mate; we might even be able to get our point across.

CHAPTER 7

EVERYONE CAN LEARN NEW SKILLS

NEW IDEAS FOR YOUR RELATIONSHIP

We fall in love and expect to live happily ever after.

Why not think this way? What's to prevent you from believing your union will last with the person you love and fighting to see it through?

We each know that our individual happiness is not enough, our partner's happiness matters, too.

We enter into a relationship knowing ourselves pretty well. To be a great mate we have to understand that our partner's happiness is vital to our own. Make their happiness a priority; not more important, equally important.

We each understand that although we love each other and are connected, we are not the same person and we have different thoughts.

Allow your special person to be just that, special; not you, not agreeing with your way of thinking, but special to his or her own way of being. If you can achieve this, you will be on your way to a great relationship.

We accept that each other has different thoughts and we don't work to change them into us.

Often we feel better when we get agreement from the one we love. It's scary being out there without someone supporting us. Learn that you don't always have to have your beloved move in lock step alongside you. You don't have to force or cajole him or her to be different. You can feel loved and be an individual in your relationship.

When we get into a disagreement we don't try to solve it when we are angry.

Use your smarts. Are you speaking kindly to the one you love when you are angry? You may be great at defending yourself or stating your case, but you are probably not speaking in kind, respectful ways. Don't try and fix a problem when you are mad. The feeling will end, (about 20 minutes, that's just plain science in our bodies) and then talk with you partner about what happened.

We solve our difficulties by talking about them and respecting ourselves and the other person's position.

Ok this is not always easy, but it is the goal. When you sit down with your mate to solve an issue I want you to remind yourself of two very important things before you begin to speak.:

1. My partner probably did not intend to hurt my feelings.

2. My partner loves me.

We are not afraid to say "I am sorry."

This one step can totally transform your relationship. Learning how to take responsibility for your "piece" and apologizing for your part in the upset by saying "I am sorry for……" It is a healing balm for you and your beloved. It also bonds you in a way that brings you closer. I know it's hard for many of us, but it's a wonderful skill to master.

We are not embarrassed to take responsibility if we were not our "best selves."

This skill relates to mending a difficulty. No one feels great about exposing a side of themselves when you know that you may have acted poorly. I know I always feel embarrassed and ashamed of myself or guilty. Most of us don't say what needs to be said because we feel those feeling too. SAY IT ANYWAY! Use your courage, walk through the embarrassment and tell you beloved person that you are sorry. Both of you will feel better.

Each of us knows that the success of both people is important to the health of the relationship.

Think of yourself as a captian of your partner's life story and achievements. You sometimes are a silent supporter, and sometimes you are a raucous cheerleader. You are the one who has the privilege to be a witness to your partner's life goals. Be a good co-captain. It's important to your partner and it will make you feel good too.

We are each other's cheerleaders, even if we do not entirely understand how our partner thinks or does things.

Sometimes we have a job and it doesn't make sense to us. Sometimes at our work we might have a difference of opinion than our boss and yet we do what the boss wants anyway. This is about the same thing. Your beloved is not us. We will not always understand why something is important to him or her. But if something is important to your partner, sense it and know that it is not your job to dampen it. If you are worried about something, explore it with open ended questions (use your starting sentence guide in the previous chapter). Remember, what your partner is interested in is important to them.

When we want something different from our partner we ask for their participation in a respectful way.

We are raised as individuals, not in a relationship. It's easy to walk into the house and see something wrong and want the mate to fix it. All of us do this. Just do it differently. Use requests, instead of demands or criticisms. And always start soft, "Honey, (or any pet name you call your beloved) would you please consider picking up your papers on the table? I would appreciate it." That's all. Don't add, "Well, when do you think you will do it? How about NOW?"

When we make a request it is up to the other person to answer it. And they could refuse to do your request. But most of us want to please the one we love and if our loved one asks us kindly to do something we will say "yes."

We don't blame or criticize to get what we want from our partner.

People grow up using blame and criticism to get what

they want. It doesn't work. It creates negativity. Use requests, they work.

We tell our mate we love them.

We may have told our beloved we loved them before. And we may believe our partner knows we love them. Sometimes I just want to know if my husband loves me in the moment. I want to know if he feels love sometimes when I am just looking at him. I am not going to remember the other times he said it to me, my wonder needs to be attended right now. Don't be stingy with your "I love yous". Be generous.

We tell our partner often that we appreciate them.

When you feel that sensation of gratitude because your loved one did something for you, don't hide it, share it! Let your special person know that you felt great when they folded the laundry. You appreciate them for the effort. Don't add, "I wish you would do it more like I have been asking." Don't spoil something with an old nag. Stay in the moment and share it with your person.

We thank them when they do something for us.

When we notice the dishes put away, or the trash taken out don't forget to say a simple thank you. It's what we teach our kids. It's what we need to hear as grown-ups. No one knows you are thinking, thank you. You must say the words. It feels good to hear.

We both want to enjoy our time on Earth together.

Saying to our mate, "We never spend time together anymore" will not bring you closer. Make a request, "Would you like to see this movie with me on Saturday?" Just ask a question, the same way you would ask a stranger. Keep it light and simple.

We make room for both of us to get what we want.

Share your ideas of life with each other. Make note of your partner's likes and dislikes, ask that they do the same for you. Share what's right for your mate, ask your partner to share what you like too.

We share the calendar and the friends, sometimes his, sometimes hers.

I do not love all my husband's friends. I love my friends. He does not love my friends, he loves his friends. Some of our friends are mutually enjoyed, not all. Share the calendar; find a way to be a supportive mate when it is not the most wonderful thing for you to do.

We respect each others original families and try to stay out of their business.

Partners think they are really good at knowing what their mates should do to solve their family issues. We always think we know exactly what would make it better. I know I always have ideas but I am very careful about sharing them. None of us will ever know the complex dynamics and history of what goes on with our mate and their families. Respect that what they have belongs to them. Be supportive to your partner, it will go a long way.

We align ourselves with our mate.

Keep in mind that you are supported and loved even when you are not with your special person. Learn how to feel their alignment with you as you go through your day, even if you don't see them. Allow them to feel this from you. You can even remind them of your devotion. Find little ways to connect. It's powerful.

We know that we have a rare thing between us, something no other two people on the planet share.

Celebrate what the two of you have together. It's incredibly unique. No other couple on the planet has the same combination of people. It only exists between the two of you. It's sacred.

We both know this is a sacred bond and we don't want to mess it up.

In our current world relationships often break. It's not uncommon for people to break-up, divorce, and end relationships. Do not be fooled that this is the inevitable way for relationships to end. Be the model for what could be. Be the love for others to see as well. That's powerful too.

We imagine what it will be like getting old with this person.

See images of you and the one you love as older people. Talk about what is funny, humorous or interesting about this journey. Not all talk about getting old has to be filled with worries.

We calm our partner's fears and their worries.

If we have worries, we share them with our partner. We don't make them our partner's worries, we just talk about them. When we talk about our worries, we worry less. Ask our partner to listen to our worries. Tell them they don't have to solve them, just listen.

We celebrate their successes.

We all need to feel valued. When we succeed we want to share it with people we love. Be your partner's better half and cheer them when they accomplish, set a new standard or reach a goal.

We ask for what we need; comfort, security, attention.

All of us have needs wants and desires. Happy couples learn how to ask for what would make them feel better, happy and safe. Healthy couples don't make it the other person's responsibility to already know what they may need. Figure it out and tell the person who loves you.

We don't pout if we are sad.

Pouting when we are sad looks really cute on a 5-year-old. It becomes pretty sad on a grown-up. Adults express what they are sad about without accusing their partner of making them so. Learn how to express your sadness. You might find a loving partner who cares about your feelings.

We express our feelings because we know our partner wants to see us happy because they love us.

When we sign up to love a person we love the whole person, feelings and all. Many people believe that they can't show any unpleasant feelings to their mate. Not so, your mate loves all of you, even the parts that are hard to show. Let your mate know your feelings. Let your partner know all of you.

We feel safe, happy and loved.

When we live here we are content. The world is good and we know we will be alright. All couples want this. I want this for you too.

These are not just ideas. These are new ways to think about how to relate to your most special person. You love your partner. That's why you are reading this book. You want to feel better in your relationship. I know you can.

CHAPTER 8

ONE MORE THING

OK, SO YOU'VE TRIED EVERYTHING AND YOU STILL FEEL like your relationship is in trouble, what now? Let's talk about learning for just a moment. You are probably very good at learning things. Chances are you went to school and learned a trade or became a professional something, learning new skills all along the way.

SAFE. HAPPY. LOVED.

When you begin to learn a new skill, do you expect to be an expert after trying one time? If you began playing an instrument would you think you would be ready to perform a concert after one or two practice sessions?

Behavioral changes are very much like learning an instrument – only the instrument is you. Because you have lived in your body all your life you expect to just tell yourself to do something different and then instantly you will know how to do it.

I wish learning new relationship skills could be instant, like flipping a light switch. But it isn't; To learn these skills requires trying them, seeing how they work, refining them and finally learning to execute them with ease.

NO ONE IS GOOD IN THE BEGINNING. There is nothing wrong with you if you feel awkward and silly doing something new. Try and remember that you are learning a new skill, like a new language, it's incredibly hard in the beginning and gets easier the more you practice.

NO one is wrong, or an idiot or stupid because you don't know how. You are simply in the process of becoming. If you can remember in the past when you learned new skills you were simply "teachable."

Become teachable again.

Try not to judge yourself and stay optimistic with the prospect of improving your relationship. It feels a whole lot better to stay enlivened with possibilities than afraid or depressed because your relationship isn't what you want.

Tell yourself you are on your way to something better. It's a journey well worth travelling.

FEELINGS CHART

In this section there are a lot of words to help you describe what you may be feeling when you get upset. We are all familiar with the words mad, bad, angry and sad. To become really skilled at describing what you are feeling, the words below can help you and your partner understand what is happening with your emotions.

Become an expert on describing how you feel something. See this as an opportunity to learn about yourself. The added benefit is that your partner will know you better, as well.

Remember, your feelings are important for two reasons; they get you relief when expressed appropriately, and they clue your mate into something that is important to you.

And don't be afraid of sounding silly when you first start expressing yourself. You will grow the muscle needed and eventually become really proficient.

Start simply with these phrases:

I felt (new word) when I heard you say what you said.

I felt (new word) when I was left out of the conference today.

I feel (new word) that we are not connecting like we used to.

I feel (new word) when you noticed I was just sitting here.

-MAD-

Annoyed   Angry   Irritated   Aggravated   Frustrated
Furious   Disgusted   Outraged   Ticked off   Fed up

-SAD-

Down   Vulnerable   Blue   Unhappy   Hurt   Depressed
Sorrowful   Discouraged   Disheartened   Disappointed
Lonely   Unloved

-BAD-

Guilty   Ashamed   Defective   Less than   Rejected
Unworthy Un-loveable Unacceptable Betrayed Helpless
Hopeless

-GLAD-

Content Satisfied Happy Thrilled Excited Ecstatic
Fulfilled Grateful Loving Peaceful Hopeful

-AFRAID-

Fearful Scared Nervous Frightened Apprehensive
Worried Terrified Unsafe Insecure Anxious Wary

REMEMBERING WHAT'S IMPORTANT

READ THIS PAGE AFTER A FIGHT TO BRING YOURSELF BACK TO THE RELATIONSHIP

My partner loves me.

My partner probably did not intend to harm me with words or actions.

Even if it feels like he or she did it on purpose I will give my mate the benefit of the doubt.

I will try and remember even when it's hard that my partner chose me and wants to be with me.

I am loved by my partner.

I will be OK.

This horrible feeling I am experiencing right now will end and I will eventually feel better.

We love each other.

I don't want to stay mad.

I don't want to make my partner the enemy.

I want to make this work.

I can make my relationship work.

Upset feelings are part of every relationship.

I will get through this.

We will be OK.

I am OK.

* 9 7 8 0 6 1 5 9 6 7 1 5 8 *